MAXIMA 120

Charles D. Richardson

Published by JamaRPublisher, LLC, Germantown, TN.
No part of this book may be reproduced in any form or by any electronic
or mechanical means including information storage and retrieval
systems currently in use or invented in the future without permission in
writing from JamaRPublisher, LLC, except by a reviewer, who may
quote brief passages in a review.

Interior Book Design by Stephanee Killen, www.integrativeink.com.
Cover Design by Angi Shearstone, Shearstone Creatives.
www.AngiShearstone.com

Library of Congress Control Number: 2009925386
ISBN-13: 978-0-9789510-1-6
ISBN-10: 0-9789510-1-8

Portions of Interviews with Madame Calment from
JEANNE CALMENT, FROM VAN GOGH'S TIME TO OURS
by Michel Allard.
English language translation copyright © 1998
by W. H. Freeman and Company.
Reprinted by arrangement with Henry Holt and Company, LLC.

Scripture taken from the HOLY BIBLE, NEW INTERNATIONAL
VERSION®, Copyright ©, 1973, 1978, 1984 by International Bible
Society. Used by permission of Zondervan Publishing House.
All rights reserved.

The "NIV" and "New International Version" trademarks are registered
in the United States Patent and Trademark Office by International
Bible Society. Use of either trademark requires the permission of
International Bible Society.

Scripture taken from The Illuminated Bible, Copyright© 1941
Columbia Educational Books, Inc.Chicago, Illinois.

Printed in La Vergne, Tennessee, USA,
by Lightning Source, Inc. on acid free paper.

Other books by this author. *The Pact*

And the Lord God said, "Behold, the man is become as one of us, to know good and evil: and now, lest he put forth his hand, and take also of the tree of life, and eat, and live for ever." Genesis 3:22

ZITS

BY JERRY SCOTT AND JIM BORGMAN

2049

WHY THE SUDDEN INTEREST IN GENETIC ENGINEERING, JEREMY?

CALL IT 'FEAR OF THE KNOWN.'

Every man desires to live long, but no man would be old.

–Jonathan Swift

Whether or not time seems to hasten or decelerate is in direct relationship to your status.

–Charles D. Richardson

Time cannot be compressed, expanded, seen, felt, controlled, bought or sold.

–Charles D. Richardson

ACKNOWLEDGMENTS AND CREDITS

It was an inspiration and great privilege to utilize passages obtained from the family Bible that belonged to my mother, Lassie Jane Richardson. Henry Holt and Company is commended for granting us the authority to use excerpts from their book *Jeanne Calment, From Van Gogh's Time to Ours*. Thanks to King Features Syndicate for the use of their March 15, 2009 ZITS feature by Jerry Scott and Jim Borgman, © 2009 ZITS Partnership, King features Syndicate.

Significant information was extracted from the files of the U.S. Department of Health and Human Services, Center for Disease Control and Prevention, National Vital Statics. Accolades go to L.Stephen Coles, M.D., Ph.D., Director of the Supercentenarian Research Foundation, who explained their rigid validation process when verifying age. Many thanks to Stephanee Killen, Integrative Ink, editor and interior design, who persevered through the making of *Maxima 120*. Last but not least, a big applause to Angi Shearstone, Shearstone Creatives, designer of the unique cover for *Maxima 120*.

AUTHOR'S NOTE

The Bible is a fascinating, mysterious, and thought-provoking book. It's crammed with complex struggles, assassinations, conspiracy, deceit, anger, jealousy, hate, revenge, hunger, adultery, homosexuality, prostitution, slavery, disease, war, and many other complex and heinous issues, not unlike our world today. At the same time, it contains among other things love, inspiration, guidance, hope, and a means of salvation. Although I have studied both the Old and New Testament rather extensively, I do not profess to be an expert by any means. In fact, I frequently encounter sentences or even entire paragraphs that seem to evoke an entirely new meaning or idea each time I study them. Neither am I a scientist, prophet, or theologian. Therefore, I have been very diligent, and hopefully I succeeded in not crossing the line when discussing God's work or laws. In these areas I strove to choose each word in order to produce a carefully worded statement or statements wherein I would remain free of blasphemy.

I wrote this book because of my interest and

fascination with God's rule that humans cannot live longer than 120 years, and yet Madame Jeanne Louise Calment apparently lived over 122 years.

MAXIMA 120

CHAPTER ONE

God created Adam and Eve with the intention of permitting them to live happily and contented in the beautiful Garden of Eden, which he provided for them. God made many species of trees that grew in the garden. Some were pleasing to the eye, and others bore fruit good for food. In the middle of the garden, he planted two special trees: the Tree of Life and the Tree of Knowledge of Good and Evil. He only demanded two things from Adam. He was to work and take care of the garden and refrain from eating fruit from the Tree of Knowledge of Good and Evil. God made it clear that he could eat fruit from any other tree in the garden, but if he violated this rule, he would surely die.

Take note that He did not forbid them from eating from the Tree of Life. I believe it would be fair to say that God intended for them to eat of the Tree of Life and live forever. If not, for what purpose did God create this tree? Of course, you may use the same logic and ask why God created a tree that Adam and Eve were forbidden to touch or whose fruits they were forbidden to consume. Perhaps he intended to let them make this critical decision for themselves. In the end, they did not have an option.

A crafty, subtle, and slick-talking snake, or Satan, convinced Eve that if she ate fruit from the Tree of Knowledge of Good and Evil she would not die but instead her eyes would open and be like God, knowing good and evil. How the serpent was able to distinguish between the Tree of Life and the Tree of Knowledge of Good and Evil is unknown. The serpent asked of Eve, "Did God really say, 'You must not eat from any tree in the garden'?"

How much time passed while Eve pondered the possibilities, weighing the pros and cons of falling for the suggestion, is not known. It may have been as short as a minute or carried out over a longer period of time. But at some point, she saw that the fruit was good for food, pleasing to her eye, and desirable for gaining wisdom. She disobeyed God and took a bite while Satan observed, presumably in a euphoric state. She wasn't naive. Either Adam or God, or possibly both, had explained the rules to her. The important thing to note here is that she knew the boundaries set by God and disobeyed. We know this because when the snake was questioning her earlier about the rules, she replied, "We may eat fruit from the trees in the garden, but God did say, 'You must not eat fruit from the tree that is in the middle of the garden, and you must not touch it, or you will die.'" In this case, God must have been referring to the Tree of Knowledge of Good and Evil and not the Tree of Life, or it's possible that Eve misquoted Him.

After Eve ate, she passed the fruit to Adam, who had been observing her interaction with the serpent and apparently kept his mouth shut—although he knew that what she had done was wrong and dangerous. Whether or not Adam wavered, procrastinated, or considered the consequences before taking a bite of the forbidden fruit is not clear. It seems as if he accepted the fruit from Eve without questioning the wisdom of doing so and ate it immediately. Then their eyes were opened, and they realized they were naked; so they sewed fig leaves together and made coverings for themselves. Their days of innocence were over. They must have immediately realized their mistake, but to no avail. They could not un-ring the bell. Their perfect existence in paradise had been turned upside down. Having knowledge of good and evil was not such a hot idea after all. They were frightened but had no one to whom they could turn. Certainly not God. So they hid among the trees and waited. Instead of slithering away, the serpent remained in the area, probably enjoying every moment of his triumph.

When confronted by God, Adam tried to take the easy way out by shifting the blame and said, "The woman you put here with me, she gave me some fruit from the tree, and I ate it," as if she had forced him to do so. Perhaps she used some feminine

3

persuasion, but there is no evidence that she pressured Adam to eat. Even so, Eve must have been stunned at his reply. Instead of protecting her, he exposed her weakness to God. Eve didn't put up a very convincing defense either, but it may have been stronger than Adam's. God said to Eve "What is this you have done?", as if he didn't already know. Eve replied, "The serpent deceived me, and I ate."

God apparently didn't hesitate to mete out punishment for the offenses. He knew what had happened before he questioned Adam and Eve. He didn't offer the serpent a chance to defend himself and said, "Because you have done this, cursed are you above all the livestock and all the wild animals! You will crawl on your belly and you will eat dust all the days of your life. And I will put enmity between you and the woman, and between your offspring and hers; he will crush your head, and you will strike his heel."

Then he admonished Eve. "I will greatly increase your pain in childbearing; with pain you will give birth to children. Your desire will be for your husband, and he will rule over you." Next came Adam's punishment. God said, "Because you listened to your wife and ate from the tree about which I commanded you, 'You must not eat of it.' Cursed is the ground because of you; through painful toil you will eat of it all the days of your life. It will produce thorns and thistles for you; and you will eat the plants of the field. By the sweat of your brow you will eat your food until you return to the ground, since from it you were taken; for dust you are and to dust you will return." Whether or not God originally intended for Adam to eventually return to dust is unknown. Adam was informed of his ultimate disposition but no time frame was imposed, only that he could not live forever.

Sometime later God spoke, presumably to an angel, and said, "The man has now become like one of us, knowing good and evil. He must not be allowed to reach out his hand and take also from the Tree of Life and eat, and live forever." To ensure that Adam and Eve would not eat from the Tree of Life and live forever, God banished them from the Garden of Eden. Adam was doomed to work the ground from which he had been taken. Apparently not fully trusting the two, and with good reason, God ensured that they would remain outside the Garden by placing cherubim and a flaming sword flashing back and forth to guard the way to the Tree of Life. By doing so God ensured that they would not have an opportunity to eat from the Tree of Life and live forever. He did not impose a maximum age to live. This would come later.

CHAPTER TWO

Initially two sons, Cain and Abel, were born to Adam and Eve. Cain tilled the soil and Abel kept flocks. They presented an offering to the Lord. Abel brought fat portions from some of the firstborn of his flock, and Cain brought some of the fruits of the soil. God preferred Abel's offering. Cain became angry and jealous of his brother, Abel, and invited him out to a field and murdered him. God punished Cain by forcing him to flee and become a restless wanderer. Cain went out from the Lord's presence and lived in the land of Nod, east of Eden.

Cain found a wife and soon their first child, Enoch, was born. Five generations are accounted for after Enoch, but Genesis is silent on the total number of issue that followed or how long they lived. However, it seems reasonable to assume that each generation had other sons and daughters who lived to a ripe old age that was customary at that time. Meanwhile, a third child named Seth was born to Adam and Eve. Adam was age 130 when Seth was born. Adam lived 930 years and was the father of other sons and daughters. How many sons and daughters Adam fathered is not known nor is the age of Eve when she died. (See Figure 6.)

When Seth was 105, he became the father of Enosh and lived another 807 years and had other sons and daughters. He died at age 912. At age 90, Enosh became the father of Kenan and lived another 815 years, fathering other sons and daughters. Altogether, Enosh lived 905 years. At age 70, Kenan became the father of Mahalalel and had other children before he died at age 910. When Mahalalel had lived 65 years, he became the father of Jared. And after he became the father of Jared, Mahalalel lived 830 years and had other sons and daughters. Altogether, Mahalalel lived 895 years. At age 162, Jared became the father of Enoch, then lived another 800 years fathering other sons and daughters. Jared lived 962 years. At age 65, Enoch became the father of Methuselah and walked with God for another 300 years. Enoch had other children and was translated at the age of 365.

Methuselah fathered Lamech at age 187 and had other children during the next 782 years, succumbing at the ripe old age of 969, the oldest recorded in history. Lamech fathered a son at age 182, named him Noah, and said, "He will comfort us in the labor and painful toil of our hands caused by the ground the Lord has cursed." Lamech lived another 595 years after Noah was born and had other sons and daughters. Lamech died at age 777. After Noah was 500 years old, he became the father of Shem, Ham, and Japheth, by far the oldest man known to father their first child.

It is interesting and ironic that the very intellect studying and exploring longevity and the aging process completely ignore our ancestors, who lived upwards of eight or nine hundred years. They generally describe today's oldest people as, "Longest living human" or "Longest confirmed lifespan in history."

Some have scoffed at the ages described in the Bible as obvious errors or the probability that years were calculated or measured in a different format than we use today. Neither of these theories will hold water if carefully examined. For instance, no evidence can be found that God had initially set an age limit on Adam and Eve. After God set the limit of 120 years in Noah's time, longevity began a modest decline until reaching His command. Afterwards longevity was measured in years less than 120, similar to a modern day centenarian. Therefore, since the ages of people gradually declined to a number that is familiar to us today, There is no logical reason to conclude that the ages listed in the Bible are anything other than what is quoted. Viewed from another angle, eight or nine hundred years is so short it is almost immeasurable on the scale of eternity.

Unfortunately, Genesis does not provide a genealogical record of females. Perhaps a reasonable assumption can be made by comparing them with today's longevity in which women live slightly longer than men. If so, they to would have lived an average of approximately 857 years. Their child bearing years are also unknown, but a strong argument could be made that they spanned many years. A case in point is Noah, who was 500 when his first child was born. However, all we know for sure is that in each generation other sons and daughters were born in addition to those mentioned. One of Cain's descendants, Lamech had two wives and had offspring by both of them. Prolonged life spans probably contributed to a population explosion.

CHAPTER THREE

And it came to pass, when men began to multiply on the face of the earth, and daughters were born unto them, that the sons of God saw the daughters of men that they were fair; and they took them wives of all which they chose. And the Lord said, "My spirit shall not always strive with man, for that he also is flesh: yet his days shall be an hundred and twenty years" (Genesis 6:1-3).

Because of the transgressions of Adam and Eve, man was forbidden to eat from the Tree of Life and live forever. Up to this time, God apparently had not set a ceiling on man's lifespan. Mankind was living on average 847.22 years. Because of their wickedness, and possibly due to the population explosion, God lowered man's maximum age to 120 years.

The Lord saw how great man's wickedness on the earth had become, and that every inclination of the thoughts of his heart was only evil all the time. The Lord was grieved that he had made man on the earth, and his heart was filled with pain. So the Lord said, "I will wipe mankind, whom I have created, from the face of the earth—men and animals, and creatures that move along the ground, and birds of the air—for I am grieved that I have made them" (Genesis 6:5-7). But Noah found favor in the eyes of the Lord. Noah was a righteous man, blameless among the people of his time, and he walked with God. God said to Noah, "I am going to put an end to all people, for the earth is filled with violence because of them. I am surely going to destroy both them and the earth." (Genesis 6:13). God explained that he was going to bring floodwaters on the earth to destroy all life except Noah, his immediate family, and a minimum of one pair of all living creatures. God instructed Noah, "So make yourself an ark of cypress wood; make rooms in it and coat it with pitch inside and out." (Genesis 6:14).

After the flood, God blessed Noah and his sons and said, "Be fruitful and increase in number and fill the earth." In God's infinite wisdom, he implemented the maximum 120 rule gradually, over a period of time. Although this command may have been reached sooner in other tribes, the Bible does not confirm an age below 121 until fourteen generations after the flood, when Joseph died at 110. Noah died at age 950.

All three sons of Noah obeyed God's command to be fruitful. Japheth was the father of seven sons, and Ham was the father of four sons. There is no mention of daughters, but surely it would be fair to say that near equal numbers of males and females were born. For instance, many generations later, Zelophehad was the father of five daughters and no sons, resulting in a special ruling by Joshua during land division in Canaan. Shem was the father of five sons and an undetermined number of daughters. From these, the nations spread out over the earth after the flood. (See Figure 6 and 6-1.)

Noah's son Shem waited two years after the flood when he was age 100 to become the father of Arphaxad. Shem lived another 500 years and became the father of other sons and daughters. When Arphaxad was 35, he became the father of Shelah. Arphaxad lived 438 years and became the father of other sons and daughters. When Shelah had lived 30 years, he became the father of Eber. Shelah lived another 403 years and became the father of other sons and daughters. At age 34, Eber became the father of Peleg. Eber lived 464 years and became the father of other sons and daughters. When Peleg had lived 30 years, he became the father of Reu. Peleg lived another 209 years and had other sons and daughters. Reu became the father of Serug at age 32. Reu lived 239 years and became the father of other sons and daughters. Serug became the father of Nahor at age 30. Serug died at age 230 and was the father of other sons and daughters.

Notice that man's lifespan continued to decline dramatically since Noah's time. At age 29, Nahor became the father of Terah, the lowest recorded to father a child up to this time. Nahor died at age 148 and was the father of other sons and daughters.

After Terah had lived 70 years, he became the father of Abram in 2166 B.C. Terah lived 205 years and was the father of three sons. God changed Abram's name to Abraham and his wife Sarai, to Sarah. In 2066 B.C., Abraham became the father of Isaac at age 100. Abraham lived another 75 years after Isaac was born and was the father of eight sons, including Ishmael, his firstborn, and Isaac.

The age at which a person was considered old had changed dramatically because Sarah, Abraham's wife, said, "Who would have said to Abraham that Sarah would nurse children? Yet I have borne him a son in his old age" (Genesis 21:7). At least Sarah considered Abraham old at age 100. Abraham's age was referred to again in Genesis 25:7-8. "Then Abraham breathed his last and died at a good old age, an old man and full of years; and he was gathered to his people." Sarah lived 127 years and was the mother of Isaac. Abraham died in 1991 B.C. after living a hundred and seventy five years. (See Figure 5 and 5-1.)

Perhaps no one could forget the incredible story of how Isaac and his beautiful wife Rebekah were brought together for marriage. Isaac was forty years old when he married Rebekah, and ten years later, they became parents of their only children, twin boys, Esau and Jacob. Isaac lived 180 years and died in 1886 B.C.

Due in part to trickery by his father-in-law, Jacob married two sisters, Leah and Rachel, although he only loved Rachel. For reasons unknown to us, God renamed Jacob, Israel. Perhaps He was preparing for the day when the Promised Land would be called Israel. Ironically, Israel and Rachel only had two children, Joseph and Benjamin.

While traveling from Padan to Bethlehem, Rachel died, to Israel's sorrow, while giving birth to Benjamin and was buried in a tomb beside a road near Bethlehem. Leah and Israel were the parents of seven children. Altogether, Israel was the father of twelve sons and Dinah, his only daughter. Israel seemed to recognize the shrinking of man's lifespan compared to his ancestors when he spoke to Pharaoh about his age and said, "The years of my pilgrimage are a hundred and thirty. My years have been few and difficult, and they do not equal the years of the pilgrimage of my fathers." Israel died in 1859 B.C. at the age 147 and was buried with Leah in a cave near Mamre with his parents, Isaac and Rebekah, and his grandparents, Abraham and Sarah.

Joseph, elder of two sons by Rachel, was disliked by some of his brothers who sold him to an Arabian merchant traveling to Egypt in a caravan. Joseph was blessed by God, resisted temptations, impressed Pharaoh with his works under God's guidance, and eventually became governor of Egypt. Joseph married Asenath, and they became the parents of two sons, Manasseh and Ephraim. During a famine in Canaan, Joseph welcomed his family to live in Egypt where food was plentiful due to his resourcefulness and God's intervention. He was not harsh to his brothers, who sold him. When Joseph's father Israel died after living seventeen years in Egypt, Joseph kept his promise and returned him to Canaan in a great procession. Joseph died in 1805 B.C. at the age of 110, the first person mentioned in the Bible that lived less than 120 years.

Moses' father and mother were Levites. Moses married Zipporah, daughter of Jethro, the priest of Midian, and they had two sons named Gershom and Eliezer. God gave Moses the task of rescuing the Israelites, who were suffering in bondage in Egypt, and return them to Canaan as promised. Moses tried unsuccessfully to convince God he was not capable of carrying out his colossal assignment. Finally, God assigned Moses' older brother, Aaron to be his spokesman—although during the next forty years Moses became his own persuasive orator.

Moses was 80 and Aaron 83 when they began negotiations with Pharaoh. After several devastating plagues befell Egypt, Pharaoh agreed to release the Israelites. As they were leaving, the Israelites plundered Egypt, taking articles of silver, gold, and clothing. Moses kept Joseph's wish and took his bones with him when the Israelites left Egypt, and they were eventually buried in the Promised Land.

During the trip to Canaan, the Israelites rebelled repeatedly and questioned the wisdom of leaving

Egypt. As punishment, God delayed their progress for forty years. Along the way, many awesome things took place. Arguably the greatest were the parting of the Red Sea, building of the tabernacle, ark and other furnishings, the pillar of cloud and the pillar of fire, and Moses' receipt of the Ten Commandments in 1445 B.C. Aaron died at age 123 on Mount Hor and Moses, the servant of God, died on Mount Nebo in 1406 B.C. at the age of 120. Neither were allowed to enter Canaan because they broke faith with God. Moses struck the rock at Meribah Kadesh for water rather than speaking to it, as instructed by God. Nevertheless, Moses was a great prophet, performed awesome deeds, and God knew him face to face.

God selected Moses' aide, Joshua to lead the Israelites. Joshua's first challenge was to cross the Jordan, which was swollen at high crest. But God applied his power as he did with the Red Sea, stopped the flow, and they crossed on the dry riverbed in 1406 B.C. Joshua was successful; he conquered and subjugated six nations and thirty-one kings after six years of war. Jericho was the first city to fall because Joshua followed God's instructions explicitly. Next, Joshua captured the nearby city of Ai. After the fall of Jericho and Ai, word spread quickly about the Israelites and their military skills; i.e., their trust in God for military guidance.

When the nearby Gibeonites heard of Joshua's success, they fabricated an elaborate ruse to trick the

Israelites into signing a peace treaty. Although their cities were nearby, the delegation arrived with well-worn clothes and sandals, cracked wine skins, and stale bread to help convince the Israelites that they had traveled a great distance. The men of Israel erred, and did not inquire of the Lord but instead sampled their provisions and swallowed the deception. Joshua made a peace treaty with the Gibeonites, and it was ratified by the assembly under oath. They quickly discovered their embarrassing error but upheld the provisions of the treaty. However, the Israelites made them wood cutters and water carriers, which were not covered in the treaty. Joshua, servant of the Lord, died at the age of 110 and was buried in the hill country of Ephraim.

CHAPTER FOUR

The average lifespan continued in a downward spiral. David was born in 1037 B.C. and died in 970 B.C. at the age of 67, similar to the life expetency in some countries today. (See Figure 5 and 5-1.) Another striking example of when people were considered elderly was during David's reign. After the death of David's rebellious son Absalom, David was met by many prominent people as he prepared to cross the Jordan on his return to Jerusalem from exile. One of David's friends was a wealthy man named Barzillai. In 2 Samuel 19:32, Barzillai is referred to as "a very old man, eighty years of age." When King David invited Barzillai to live with him in Jerusalem, Barzillai reflected his thoughts on age and its afflictions by replying, "How many more years will I live, that I should go up to Jerusalem with the king? I am now eighty years old. Can I tell the difference between what is good and what is not? Can your servant taste what he eats and drinks? Can I still hear the voices of men and women singers? Why should your servant be an added burden to my lord the king?" Barzillai's assessment of his infirmities are very similar to many modern day people at age 80.

Aristotle, born in 384 B.C., died in 322 B.C. at 62. Herod the Great was born in 73 B.C. and died in 4 B.C. at the age of 69. Constantine the Great was born A.D. 272. and died A.D. 337 at the age of 65. Herod Antipas, Herod the Great's son, was born 20 B.C. and died A.D. 39 at the age of 59, living ten years less than his father.

Flavius Claudius Constantinus, son of Constantine I, a Roman Emperor, was born A.D. 317 and died A.D. 340 at the age of 23. Saint Bede, an English Monk, author and scholar, was born A.D. 673 and died A.D. 735 at the age of 52. King Alfred the Great, cherished and admired by his subjects, was born A.D. 849 and died A.D. 899 at the age of 50.

Saint Francis of Assisi, born into a wealthy Italian family, devoted most of his life to helping the poor. Because of this he was an outcast from family and friends. He overcame all hardships and eventually became successful in amassing large sums of money that he devoted to the poor. He died A.D. 1226 at the age of 35.

The famous explorer and author, Marco Polo, died A.D. 1324 at the age of 70, a rather old age for that era. Geoffrey Chaucer, an English philosopher and author perhaps best known for *The Canterbury Tales,* died A.D. 1400 at the age of 55. Christopher

Columbus died A.D 1506 also at the age of 55.

Fifty-eight years after Columbus's death, Galileo was born, and he survived for 78 years, seemingly setting a new trend. A year after Galileo's death in A.D. 1642, Isaac Newton was born and lived 84 years. Ben Franklin died in 1790, also at the age of 84. Nine years later, George Washington died at 57. Charles Babbage, who originated the concept of programmable computing, died in 1871 at the age of 79. Louis Pasteur died in 1895 at the age of 73. Florence Nightingale, well known for her work in nursing care improvement, died in 1910 at the age of 90, and last but not least, Winston Churchill, famous for his leadership as Prime Minster during the United Kingdom's struggle in World War II, died in 1965 at 91.

These famous people outlived the average person by several years despite the likelihood that most of them led a soft lifestyle with minimum exercise and an over indulgence in rich food. Shockingly, the U.S. life expectancy in 1900 for the average Joe was only 46, and 48 for his spouse. (See Figures 8 and 9.)

CHAPTER FIVE

Starting in 1900, the U.S. government began a mammoth program to collect and record vital statistics based on age-specific death rates. In 1900, only 0.03 percent survived to age 100 compared to 3.6 percent by the year 2002. Only 87.6 percent of infants survived the first year compared to a 99.3 percent survival rate in 2002. These positive advances can be primarily attributed to improved education, nutrition, sanitation, and recent remarkable medical achievements.

These statistics were broken down to dramatize the differences in male, female, and in some cases race. Life expectancy is steadily increasing at closely the same rate for both white and black people in the U.S. Between 1970 and 1982, the life expectancy of white females climbed at a rate of 0.166666666 per year, then decreased to 0.15 between 1982 and 2002. The other three categories increased at a similar rate for the past 20 years. At this rate, white females would reach a life expectancy of 120 years in 2262. (See Figure 1.)

According to the National Vital Statistics Reports, life expectancy of white females increased from 80.2 in 2001 to 80.3 in 2002. At this slightly slower rate, the 120 mark would not be reached until 2402. It's interesting to note in Figure 1 that in 1900, white males were expected to live longer than black females until age 72. At this juncture, a crossover is made and life expectancy for black females slightly exceeds that of white males.

By age 100, there is very little difference between the white and black populations in terms of survival. Somewhat less than 1 percent of white and black males and about 2.6 percent of white and black females survive to age 100. (See Figure 11.)

CHAPTER SIX

One of God's promises to the Israelites was a full life span, provided they obey his laws and commands. "I will give you a full life span" (Exodus 23:26.) God did not identify what He meant by "full life span," but it would eventually become 120 years or less.

I think it would be fair to say that most if not all people want an extended life cycle. As in most things in life, there are exceptions because of such troublesome interactions as mental, social, and economic problems that confront us. Thus, people sometimes commit suicide because of divorce, huge financial losses, or loss of a loved one. Fortunately, these are the exception and only comprise a small portion of the population.

The majority prefers to push the outer boundaries of the life cycle as far as possible. As early as 440 B.C., during Herodotus' travels, he mentions a special fountain in Ethiopia and attributes the perceived longevity of the Ethiopians to this water.

And of course, Ponce de León scoured over Florida in search of the elusive fountain of youth.

People pursue the fountain today but in a different manner. Promoting youth, or more correctly a less elderly appearance, is big business. Cosmetic plastic surgeons do quite well performing facial rejuvenation, tummy tucks, laser skin resurfacing, and reshaping just about any body part you can imagine. Of course, these operations are not advertised nor intended to increase longevity but to improve a person's appearance. However, there is a strong possibility that by improving one's self image, a spin-off could be an increased life span.

CHAPTER SEVEN

$\mathcal{S}$ome scientists believe the body has a built-in time clock that ultimately determines how long a particular human will live. That's probably an over-simplification of the aging process. It's been widely known for many years that a group of small organs located within the torso and head, together known as the endocrine system, acts as the staging grounds for body functions. Some of the more recognizable organs, known as endocrine glands, are the pituitary, thyroid, ovary, and testes. These glands release hormones. Hormones have a dramatic effect on the body's growth rate, determines puberty, mood, and most important, regulates tissue function and metabolism. Metabolism is a word used to describe necessary chemical reactions within living organisms that promote growth and reproduction.

A very important function of metabolism is the conversion of energy into cell parts, such as nucleic acids and proteins. If an endocrine gland didn't trigger this process and metabolism didn't occur in a particular instance, then the cell would not be repaired and it would die. A great mystery is what force influences or triggers the glands to release hormones. And just as perplexing is how the glands are able to deliver the correct quantity of hormones. The pituitary gland, about the size of a bean, is located in the brain. It is the master gland, a gate-keeper that turns the others on and off as needed. It also triggers the release of endorphins into the bloodstream. Endorphins are released by factors such as vigorous exercise, extended laughter, and eating certain foods, such as dark chocolate. When the endorphins enter the blood stream, it triggers a euphoric state, a calm feeling of well-being, commonly known as "runners-high." Each individual is affected to a slightly different degree by the endorphins. But one must ask, what activates the controlling gland? Since the pituitary gland is connected to the brain, there is a probability that it receives its signals from the brain.

Inside each of the estimated 100 trillion cells that make up our body are 46 chromosomes, except for the reproduction cells, which contain only 23. Females have 23 chromosomes in their reproductive cells and males have 23 in their sperm cells, for a total of 46, just like other cells in our body. A chromosome is a long, single piece of coiled DNA containing over 4,000 tiny, spiral-like objects called genes. Most people are familiar with the term because our genes are forwarded from parent to offspring and determine important things about us, such as the color of our eyes and hair. Some molecular scientists believe that a small number of genes play an important role in the aging process.

A gene is a portion of deoxyribonucleic acid (DNA). DNA has the uncanny ability to instruct a gene how and when to function, similar to a chemical message delivered by the endocrine system. If enough genes become unable to function, for whatever reason, catastrophic things can happen to our body. For example, if enough genes in our brain cells cease to function or fail to function at the expected level, our ability to carry on in a normal manner may be impaired. Our ability to reason may slow or diminish. Likewise, if certain genes that control cell growth malfunction, the result can be a cancerous growth.

Regardless of all the knowledge gained in the recent past about God's remarkable creation, the question remains what triggers the cell growth malfunction, or why do genes become unable to function? Whether man will ever know the answer to these far-reaching questions, and be able to intervene, is anyone's guess. Have you ever wondered how a seed in the ground knows when to sprout? Or in complete darkness, how it determines in which direction to grow in order to reach sunlight? Or how a leaf or flower turns during the day to follow and catch the preponderance of sun rays? Certainly something inside plants and seeds initiates and coordinates this activity. Perhaps their system is similar to and just as mysterious as ours. An unlimited amount of miraculous things on earth and in the universe simply cannot be easily explained by mortal man.

We have no control over who our natural parents are and thus no control over the genes we inherit. It's common knowledge that outside influences help shape our longevity. Our genes have remained the same for eons, forwarding their built-in codes from one generation to the next, but as we have seen, longevity in the U.S. has steadily risen since the 1900s. Outside influences are responsible for these changes, some dramatically. Commonly known influences that have increased our longevity are improvements in the medical field, sanitation, and nutrition.

On the other hand, there are some well known and controllable outside influences that have hindered longevity. Among those confronting the U.S. and other developed nations today are obesity, lack of exercise, poor eating habits—such as dependence on fast foods and soft drinks—drugs, and tobacco products. It's an established fact that exercising regularly, controlling weight, proper nutrition, and an affinity with God is a guaranteed way to increase longevity. Not only does it increase longevity but also the added years will be more enjoyable. One could only speculate where the average lifespan would be today if every American had followed the golden rules of living since the 1900s.

CHAPTER EIGHT

In the early eighties, the United States Government, under the auspices of the Department of Energy and later the United States National Institute of Health, undertook an awesome project tasked to gain an understanding of the human genome. By 1990, enough interest in the project had been generated in the United States and several other developed countries that Congress authorized three billion dollars to get the project off the ground. Known as the Human Genome Project (HGP), its primary mission was to identify and map the human genome and determine the sequence of chemical base pairs which make up DNA.

The project proceeded quicker than originally thought due to international cooperation and improved computer technology. Thirteen years later, the project was more than 90 percent complete but has made very little progress since. Some scientists believe new technology must be developed before the remainder of the unique human genome can be sequenced.

A very controversial aspect of the human genome research is the prospect of genetic engineering and destruction of an embryo when stem cells are removed. These controversial and emotional issues have resonated up to the White House for decision-making. As the term "engineering" implies, the idea is to amend DNA by modifying the genes of a human egg, sperm, or young embryo to obtain sought after traits and to treat diseases. Scientists believe they could uncover improved treatment or possibly a cure for such debilitating diseases as diabetes and Alzheimer's. Repairing spinal cord injuries are also in the offing. Some scientists believe stem cells have the capability to evolve into any organ or tissue cell in the human body. Changes to genes in the unborn would be permanent and forwarded to the next generation.

Opponents of embryonic stem cell research argue that human life is destroyed during the experiments. Supporters of the process counter that the frozen embryonic cells obtained from fertility clinics are surplus cells generated during in vitro fertilization and would be discarded if not used for research. How many, if any, are discarded is unknown. Most likely, the majority are frozen awaiting their ultimate destination.

During the George W. Bush administration, federal funds were virtually frozen for embryonic stem cell research. Private research was carried out during the Bush reign but at a much slower pace than if the U.S. government had provided funds. The

Obama administration reversed this policy in early 2009. The National Institute of Health moved expeditiously in developing guidelines for the use of federal funding for embryonic stem cell research. The guidelines, if adopted, will allow research on leftover embryos not used by fertility clinics. Federal funds would be withheld for embryos created by therapeutic cloning or for other research.

Alternate methods have been developed that do not utilize embryonic stem cells. Stem cells from adult tissue and umbilical cords have been used in the treatment of spinal cord injuries and multiple sclerosis. Another discovery during the Bush administration is the so-called, induced pluripotent stem cells. This procedure injects genes into a skin cell. The results are advertised as having the same pluripotent qualities of embryonic stem cells. Some scientists believe that adult stem cells are vulnerable to inaccurate reproduction and could lose a tiny fraction of genetic information each time the cell divides. Scientists seem to universally agree that embryonic stem cells are the gold standard because of their ability to divide almost indefinitely and produce every type of cell in the human body.

The genes of each individual, except identical twins, are unique, just as fingerprints are unique. Genetic tests can be made to determine a person's likelihood of acquiring a variety of illnesses, such as liver disease, breast cancer, and cystic fibrosis. Coupled with this knowledge, an individual would be better prepared when making difficult decisions as to what course of action to take in respect to the management of a potential illness.

In turn, this information has caused controversy in some quarters who argue that the data could be obtained by outside agencies, such as insurance companies who might use the information in making critical decisions on insurability. Others argue that genetic engineering might primarily benefit the well connected or wealthy because of its cost. A super society of genetic aristocracy could arise and widen the chasm between the haves and the have-nots and create a social upheaval.

So, why are we discussing the very fabric of the human body? The answer is because it is believed that the knowledge gained by the HGP project will lead to new frontiers in medicine and biotechnology. The basic premise is the desire to increase our life span and improve our ability to be active and enjoy the extra time. How and if we get there will probably be debated for many years to come and remain a very emotional aspect in our lives as we try to determine if the benefits of healing and relief from suffering outweighs the religious implications.

There is some speculation that another controllable way to increase your life expectancy is to live in certain parts of the world that seem to be conducive to longevity. In Dan Buettner's new release, *Blue Zones*, he identifies locations on earth where people are living longer. One location, Loma

Linda, California, is near Los Angeles where Gertrude Baines lives. She just happens to be the oldest living person on earth as of this writing. She will be 116 on April 6, 2010. She was born in Georgia and lived in several locations including Canada, Connecticut, and Ohio before moving to Los Angeles. So it is questionable if living near Loma Linda could be attributed to her longevity. Another case is Christian Mortensen, who lived to age 115. He also lived the latter part of his life in California. Most likely the primary factors that account for their longevity can be attributed to well known traits, such as favorable genes, medical treatment, lifestyle, and nutrition.

Japan has an estimated 36,000 centenarians. The Japanese enjoy a life expectancy of 81.25 years compared to 77.8 in the United States.

CHAPTER NINE

As stated in chapter three, God gradually lowered the 120 maximum age limit. The first recorded death at or below the age of 120 was Joseph, who died at the age of 110. Moses died at the age of 120. The Bible isn't clear as to how many days Moses lived after his one hundred and twentieth birthday, only that he didn't live to see his one hundred and twenty-first birthday.

At some point in time after Aaron's death, Moses was told by God that he was to die and would not be allowed to enter the Promised Land. No doubt this was devastating news after all the suffering and hard work Moses had invested in the Israelites. He had struggled forty years with the sometimes unruly and ungrateful Israelites, taking them from bondage in Egypt to the entrance to the Promised Land. However, he probably suspected that his fate was sealed, similar to his brother Aaron's. At Mount Hor, God had spoken to Aaron and Moses saying, "Aaron will be gathered to his people. He will not enter the land I give the Israelites, because both of you rebelled against my command at the waters of Meribah." (Numbers 20, 20:23.) Regardless, Moses pleaded with God, "Let me go over and see the good land beyond the Jordan—that fine hill country and Lebanon." (Deuteronomy 3:25.) God refused to bargain with Moses and replied matter-of-factly, "That is enough. Do not speak to me anymore about this matter." (Deuteronomy 3:26.)

Moses was told he would climb Mount Nebo, where he could view the Promised Land before dying. How much time lapsed after Moses was advised of his fate and his death notice is unknown. However, it must have been quite some time because God told Moses that he was to "Take vengeance on the Midianites for the Israelites. After that you will be gathered to your people." After a successful campaign against Midian, Moses assembled all of the tribes and reviewed their incredible journey from Egypt, read the Ten Commandments to them, then wrote the Book of Law. As his final act, all tribes were assembled and received his blessings.

He must have been in reasonably good health for his age. Moses was not feeble because he had enough stamina to climb from the Plains of Moab to the summit of 2,624-foot Mount Nebo. His eyes were not weak because he could see the whole land as far as the western sea. The closest point to the Mediterranean is approximately 62 miles west of Mount Nebo. Was God standing firm on his word after permitting Aaron to live three years past the maximum permissible age of 120?

CHAPTER TEN

On February 21, 1996, 3,402 years after Moses' death in 1406 B.C., a very remarkable and earth shaking event occurred. As far as we know, God kept his decree since Moses' death to limit our longevity to a maximum of 120 years. However, all indications are that a French woman named Jeanne Louise Calment reached the age of 121 years on February 21, 1996. Technically speaking, she exceeded God's rule 120 years and one second after the instant of her birth in 1875. But we know that Moses' death was not at the exact instant he reached 120 years. His death was after his 120th birthday but prior to reaching his 121st birthday. So I used the same logic in determining when Mrs. Calment exceeded the 120-year rule.

Mrs. Calment was born on February 21, 1875 and died August 4, 1997 at the age of 122 years and 164 days. This is based on the assumption that all the man-made records used to calculate her age are correct. The documentation used to determine her age seems to be flawless and airtight. According to the official records, Mrs. Calment was born in Arles, France and lived there her entire life. The records of her birth, baptism, marriage, death, and the census seem to be infallible and have produced more documentation than any other super centenarian.

The following is a partial quote from L. Stephen Coles, M.D., Ph.D., Director of the Super Centenarian Research Foundation in Inglewood, California: "We have documented the age of French *Guinness Book of World Records* holder Madam Jeanne-Louise Calment at her death on August 4, 1997 at age 122 years, 164 days through several sources, including her personal physician, interviews with scientific researchers who studied her before she died, and our Gerontology Research Group representative at that time, Professor Jean-Marie Robine, Ph.D. of Montpelier, France. Our validation methodology includes the acquisition of at least three pieces of official documentation, including a birth or baptismal certificate, marriage certificate with an audit trail for women's maiden names and some sort of photo identification or passport to preclude an imposter from using someone else's documentation as their own."

Mrs. Calment was the youngest child born into a family in which some members were blessed with long lifespans. Nothing like hers but nevertheless quite noteworthy for that era. Her brother Francois lived 97 years; her mother, Marguerite Gilles, lived

86 years; and her father, Nicolas, lived to age 93. Her ancestors must have been blessed with a very strong immune system. They weathered many hardships almost unscathed, such as plagues, cholera epidemics, and extreme food shortages nearing a famine. The majority of her ancestors had a long life span. Mrs. Calment survived a cholera outbreak at age 9, the plague at age 25, and the flu pandemic at 43. Whether or not Madame Calment's family fled to one of her father's farms to escape these deadly diseases is unknown. On the down side, her oldest brother Antoine died at age 4, and her older sister Marie died at age 3, possibly the result of one or more of these scourges.

Obviously Mrs. Calment inherited genes with a propensity for long life. Also in her favor is the strong tendency for people who live in Southern France to have a life expectancy that is among the highest in the world. Mrs. Calment spent her entire life in Arles, which is located in Southern France. Some have attributed this phenomenon to their diet, which includes red wine and olive oil. Scientific research has proven that red wine and olive oil contains ingredients that are conducive to a long lifespan. Extra virgin olive oil contains high levels of monounsaturated fat and antioxidative substances. Possible benefits from these two ingredients range from weight control, cancer inhibitor, reduced likelihood of heart disease, diabetes control, reduced incidence of osteoporosis, and a lowered risk of colon cancer. Madame Calment used olive oil extensively by spreading it on most of her food and rubbed it into her skin.

Red wine contains flavonoids that among other substances act as an antioxidant similar to olive oil. Antioxidants are compounds that protect cells against the damage of oxidative stress, which is associated with many diseases and aging. Dark chocolates are also rich in flavonoids, and Madame Calment consumed a considerable amount of chocolate. Madame Calment was fond of seafood and regularly traveled with her husband Fernand some 60 miles to Marseille, located on the southern coast, and is noted among other things for their famous sea food.

Sadly as well as perplexing, her only child, Yvonne, and only grandchild, Frederic Billot, both died at age 36. Yvonne died from pneumonia and Frederic died from a tragic automobile accident. Frederic did not father any children. Neither did her brother Francois. The untimely and tragic death of Frederic, who had become a physician specializing in ear, nose and throat, brought the line of Madame Calment to a sad conclusion. Whatever the special ingredient or spark she carried in her genes for over 122 years was forever lost.

Mrs. Calment's father was a successful shipbuilder and her husband, Fernand, inherited a large fabric store that was very profitable and employed several people. They were not ultra rich but lived quite comfortably and were able to afford a servant when they were first married. Consequently she wasn't strapped down with mundane household work and was able to pursue a rather ideal lifestyle, engaging in such physical activities as tennis, swimming, cycling, walking, and hunting with her husband. When asked about working at a job she replied, "Oh well, that doesn't mean a thing to me! I wasn't encouraged." Did she imply that had she been encouraged she would have worked outside her home? At a later interview, she somewhat recanted her earlier statement and said, "Well, yes, I would have liked to. To be useful." One could easily speculate that had Madame Calment been encouraged to work, or if she had been born in 1975 instead of 1875, she very well might have become the CEO of a major corporation.

She was very active at age 100. Incredibly, she recounts running throughout Arles on her 100th birthday to thank her friends and family for the flowers they had sent her. These are activities that tend to extend one's life. She did engage in one activity that normally curtails longevity. Madame Calment revealed that her husband introduced her to cigarettes. When asked when she started smoking she responded, "When I got married, not before, my father wouldn't have wanted it." At that time the dangers of tobacco use was not generally known. Fernand loved Mrs. Calment and surely didn't realize the deadly consequences of a social cigarette after dinner. Mrs.

Calment eventually became addicted and normally smoked two cigarettes or cigarillos a day until she was 119. She developed a chronic cough later in life that was attributed to her smoking habit. However, she avoided some of the horrible results of smoking, such as lung and throat cancer.

She was an attractive though diminutive woman. In her earlier life, she was a picture of health, with a full head of brunette hair, wide-set gray eyes, high cheekbones covered with fair skin, and complimented with a Mona Lisa smile.

During her extended lifetime, many significant events occurred. She was 23 when Wilbur Wright was flitting around the sky, demonstrating the Wright Flyer to a stunned crowd at Le Mans. At 39, she witnessed the beginning of World War I, the deadliest war in human history. A few years later, France and Germany plunged into World War II. At 94, she witnessed the historic journey of Neil Armstrong and Buzz Aldrin to the moon and made it known that she, too, would like to travel to the moon.

CHAPTER ELEVEN

For argument's sake, let's assume that the official government and church records of Arles are correct. No mistakes or erroneous entries, intended or otherwise. This begs the question of why God allowed Mrs. Calment to exceed his 120-year rule. Was she a unique person chosen by God and used for a purpose that has not yet been revealed? If not, has God amended or cancelled the rule? These are questions to which, undoubtedly, none of us has a plausible answer at this time—questions that will, most likely, be pondered in the future by scientists and theologians. Mrs. Calment acknowledged her unusual standing when she pondered on different occasions: "I've been forgotten by a good God." "He's forgotten me." "The good Lord must have forgotten me."

Because God is omni-present and aware of all events on earth and the universe, even the number of hairs on our head, I don't think for a second He forgot about Mrs. Calment. Perhaps God did amend or cancel His 120 rule. After all, we know that under certain compelling circumstances, God has changed his mind. For instance, in Exodus 32, while Moses was on Mount Sinai obtaining the Ten Commandants, the Israelites became dissatisfied and asked Aaron to make them gods. Surprisingly, Aaron complied and made a gold calf from their jewelry. The next day the people sacrificed burnt offerings and presented fellowship offerings. After eating and drinking they indulged in revelry. God knew what they were up to and instructed Moses to leave the mountain after explaining that the Israelites were corrupt and were worshiping an idol cast in the shape of a calf.

"I have seen these people," the Lord said to Moses, "and they are a stiff-necked people. Now leave me alone so that my anger may burn against them and that I may destroy them. Then I will make you into a great nation." (Exodus 32:9-10.)

But instead of leaving God alone, Moses stubbornly sought the favor of the Lord his God. He pleaded with God that the Egyptians would proclaim that the removal of the Israelites from Egypt was for evil intent to kill them in the mountains.

Another matter Moses mentioned was God's promise to Abraham, Isaac, and Israel concerning the Promised Land and its Israelite inhabitants becoming as numerous as the stars in the sky. If he destroyed the Israelites, he would not be able to carry out his promise to the three patriarchs. Moses adjured God saying, "Turn from your fierce anger, relent and do not bring disaster on your people." (Exodus 32:12.) After hearing Moses' counter, God relented and refrained from destroying the Israelites.

In 1 Kings 21, God sent judgment against Ahab, King of Israel, and his wife Jezebel for their treachery against Naboth, who owned a vineyard that Ahab desired. Naboth refused both of Ahab's offers of another vineyard in exchange or to purchase Naboth's vineyard. While Ahab sulked because of Naboth's rejection, Jezebel designed and implemented a plan to have Naboth stoned for allegedly cursing Ahab and God. Her plan worked, and Naboth was stoned to death. Ahab proceeded to take possession of the vineyard when he was told that Naboth was dead. Whether he simply seized the vineyard or paid for it is not clear. God declared through the Prophet Elijah that disaster would befall Ahab but changed his mind after Ahab became repentant.

The Lord instructed the Prophet Elijah, say to King Ahab, "In the place where dogs licked up Naboth's blood, dogs will lick up your blood—yes, yours."

Ahab said to Elijah, "So you have found me, my enemy!"

"I have found you," Elijah replied. "Because you have sold yourself to do evil in the eyes of the Lord. The Lord said, 'I am going to bring disaster on thee. I will consume your descendants and cut off from Ahab every last male in Israel—slave and free. I will make your house like that of Jeroboam son of Nebat and that of Baasha son of Ahijah, because you have provoked me to anger and have caused Israel to sin.'"

Elijah continued, "Dogs will devour Jezebel by the wall of Jezreel.

"Dogs will eat those belonging to Ahab who die in the city, and the birds of the air will feed on those who die in the country."

When Ahab heard Elijah's pronouncement, he tore his clothing, put on sackcloth, and fasted. He lay in sackcloth and went around meekly.

Then the word of the Lord came to Elijah, "Have you noticed how Ahab has humbled himself before me? Because he has humbled himself, I will not bring this disaster in his day, but I will bring it on his house in the days of his son."

In Exodus 33, God changed his mind again. After Moses destroyed the golden calf and heavily disciplined the Israelites for their sinful ways, God told Moses to proceed to the Promised Land, the land flowing with milk and honey. The Lord told Moses he would send an angel ahead of him to drive out the inhabitants. Then he added, "But I will not go with you, because you are a stiff-necked people and I might destroy you on the way." Moses responded, "You have been telling me, 'Lead these people,' but you have not let me know whom you will send with me. You have said, 'I know you by name and you have found favor with me.' If you are pleased with me, teach me your ways so I may know you and continue to find favor with you. Remember that this nation is your people." The Lord changed his mind and replied to Moses, "My presence will go with you, and I will give you rest." Moses replied, as if he had misunderstood what God said or perhaps he just wanted reassurance, "If your Presence does not go with us, do not send us up from here. How will anyone know that you are pleased with me and with your people unless you go with us? What else will distinguish me and your people from all the other people on the face of the earth?" The Lord said to Moses, "I will do the very thing you have asked, because I am pleased with you and I know you by name."

Another example of God's way is located in Samuel II after David takes a census of men capable of military service. Because of the census, God advised David through the prophet Gad, "Go and say unto David, Thus saith the Lord, I offer thee three things; choose thee one of them, that I may do it unto thee." So Gad came to David, and told him, and said unto him, "Shall seven years of famine come unto thee in thy land? Or wilt thou flee three months before thine enemies, while they pursue thee? Or that there be three day's pestilence in thy land? Now advise, and see what answer I shall return to Him that sent me."

Instead of choosing one of the three choices, David eliminated one when he replied to Gad, "I am in a great strait: let us fall now into the hand of the Lord; for his mercies are great: and let me not fall into the hand of man."

David was apparently reticent and didn't select one of the three choices, so the Lord made the selection for him and sent an angel with a pestilence upon Israel, killing seventy thousand men from Dan to Beersheba. But when the angel stretched out his hand upon Jerusalem to destroy it, the Lord repented him of the evil, and said to the angel, "It is enough: stay now thine hand." At some point after the pestilence began, Gad advised David to build an altar unto the Lord. David complied, built an altar, and offered burnt offerings and peace offerings. So the Lord was entreated for the land, and the plague was stayed from Israel. How many hours passed after the pestilence begun and the completion of the offerings by David is unknown, but presumably, many lives were saved by God's early withdrawal of the pestilence.

In 2 Kings 20:1–6, Hezekiah became King of Judea, the southern half of what was at one time Israel. He was 25 when he became king. He trusted and did what was right in the eyes of the Lord, which was a reversal from what most of his ancestors had practiced. He destroyed all the man-made gods in Judea, including the bronze snake made by Moses because people were burning incense to it. At the young age of 29, Hezekiah became gravely ill. The prophet Isaiah visited Hezekiah and said, "This is what the Lord says: 'Put your house in order, because you are going to die; you will not recover.'" Hezekiah turned his face to the wall and prayed to the Lord, "Remember O Lord how I have walked before you faithfully and with wholehearted devotion and have done what is good in your eyes." And Hezekiah wept bitterly. Before Isaiah had left the middle court, the word of the Lord came to him: "Go back and tell Hezekiah, the leader of my people, 'This is what the Lord, the God of your father David says: I have heard your prayer and seen your tears; I will heal you. On the third day from now you will go up to the temple of the Lord. I will add fifteen years to your life.'"

God changed his mind and added fifteen years to Hezekiah's life, which extended it to age 54. As a bonus, God promised Hezekiah he would defend Jerusalem from the aggressive army of Assyria, who had been threatening to overthrow that great city.

If God relaxed or cancelled His maximum 120 rule, one must speculate not only why but when. If a revision or revisions were made, presumably they would occur prior to the time that Mrs. Calment exceeded the original time limit. If He cancelled the original rule, did He set another time limit? And if so, what is the revised limit and how will we know? Another perplexing dilemma could arise if humans are allowed to, and many actually do exceed the 120 rule. The social and economic impact could be overwhelming. Will they be able to care for themselves into what is considered today an advanced age with dignity? Will they work longer, depriving a younger generation of jobs? Will medical care and Social Security be able to accommodate thousands of super seniors? Mrs. Calment's life would seem to dispel most of these worries, but then she was a very unique woman.

CHAPTER TWELVE

At the last moment, I decided to add this chapter devoted entirely to the extraordinary life of Madame Jeanne Louise Calment. She maintained a lifestyle until the end that could set the high standards needed for anyone interested in elevating their life to an advanced level, fulfilled with enjoyment and peace. Not that Madame Calment's life was entirely perfect. It wasn't. Regardless, she somehow managed to persevere, to maintain a positive outlook and sunny disposition that surely helped carry her over the rough spots in her life, in which there were many. She viewed life philosophically and only waivered slightly from this perspective near the end.

Madame Calment was close to 115 when she fell and injured herself. Up to that point, she would begin her day with exercise designed to keep her joints flexible. After her exercise, she said her daily prayer. Perhaps there is no better way to describe her life than that of her own words.

Following is a series of interviews between

Madame Calment and her friend and physician, Doctor Victor Lebre, conducted at her retirement home, Maison du Lac. This dialogue, taken from *Jeanne Calment From Van Gogh's Time to Ours*, occurs shortly after her 118th birthday.

How old are you now?
"One hundred and eighteen."

Are you happy about that?
"Well! Of course! We don't all get there."

But you know that we have a bet, both of us?
"What's that?"

That you will reach one hundred and twenty years old.
"Oh!"

Will you be happy to reach one hundred and twenty years old?
"Well, of course! Because I will have the time to make the most of loads of things to come, loads of interesting things."

What are you interested in now?
"Oh! Well, all, all and nothing."

So, you know that I have a pact with you, to reach one hundred and twenty years of age?

"Ah! That I doubt!'"

You don't believe in medicine?
"Yes, but I don't believe in yours much! It's to reassure you."

You think it's to reassure myself that I say that?
"Yes."

"We will go together as far as 120!
"This pact is actually to reassure you more than me; I'm not afraid of dying but with you it's different."

You don't fear death then?
"Oh, what am I doing? I've lost my parents, I've lost my children. What do you want? I live. When I am not suffering; physically I don't suffer, so I let myself live. I live mechanically."

You're not afraid of dying?
"No. Now, I wish for it, as life holds no interest for me."

It makes me happy that you are there.
"The pleasure is shared. It reassures me to hear you."

That's nice, and I am very happy to see you.
"Ah! You won't see me for much longer."

How are you now, after the party?
"I'm very well. Very well, very well."

I saw a photo of you in the paper when you were young, and you looked marvelous.
"Ah! When one is young, one is beautiful! But it's the beauty of youth; it's the sign of youth."

That's how you got to be 118 years old?
"Ha! Ha! You're just talking. I just came to be like that: I did nothing, I have a good appetite. I don't worry about anything. I'm lucky. They say rascals are lucky! I must be a big one!"

How are you?
"Well, I'm not getting anywhere; I'm still not getting anywhere."

Before being 100, did you think about it?
No. But I know how to live. I was living. I made the most of life."

And do you remember your hundredth birthday?
"What the devil, at 100! Friends and family sent flowers and I went to them in town to say thank you. Running! I ran! At 100, I was running."

What are you thinking about?
"The future, I think my end is near."

Shortly before Christmas, Doctor Lebre asked her, *So what should I get as gifts?*

"Ah, it's difficult to say. It's up to you. Books, lovely books, reading, magazines, lovely books mostly, reading."

Interview between Madame Calment and Doctor Lebre soon after her 119th birthday.

How are you?

"My memory is asleep. So many things have happened in my life that one takes over where the other leaves off. I think one day at a time that I'm going to die. I know that I'm going to die."

Are you thinking about the year 2000?

"I don't think about it since I'm leaving it. I'm leaving it."

How do you see the future?

"Oh! Very well. I've lived enough. I will go willingly."

But you still want to be alive all the same?

"Still, yes. But not like before. Whatever God wants."

You are tired?

"Well! Tired isn't the word. I am tireless! Tired, that's not the right word."

"I promised that I'd live to 120 years; I'll do my best."

What about God?
"He's forgotten me. He can't be in a hurry to see me. He already knows me very well. Death doesn't frighten me; I can think peacefully of ending a long life."

What do you wish for a gift?
"Oh! A beautiful book, by a good author. There are so many good authors; there is no shortage of them. I was very gifted in the arts."

What school did you go to?
"Wait . . . Madame Benet's boarding school, it was a church school. I had my first communion there."

And then what school did you go to?
"Oh, well, there was college. It was on the Lices."

You never wanted to work in your entire life?
"No, my parents encouraged me to cultivate the arts—music, painting. I had an aptitude as much for one as the other. I loved painting. I loved music. I loved all that and very tasteful."

Did the birth of your daughter go well?

"Very well. Yes, it went normally, and at home in my bedroom in Arles. You didn't go to the hospital in those days. You gave birth at home. With the midwife. The midwife was a woman, Madame Leliere. Madame Leliere was very capable. She helped me give birth. It went very well, it was easy. She was capable, she was the best woman. I had a constitution that lent itself very well to that, I helped a lot. I gave birth alone like everything I do. Right away, so it would be over with."

And your mother, what was her name?
"Marguerite . . . She was charming, sweet. She was an Arlesian, sweet, smart. Oh! Very gentle."

She spoiled you, too?
"Oh, a lot! I was very spoiled, very."

So your parents loved you very much?
"Very much. I was their pride and joy."

Her father Nicolas amassed several farms near Arles, which produced wine, goat cheese, and several different crops. Madame Calment loved to visit the farms as a child. Her husband was an avid hunter and taught Madame Calment the sport. She developed such a love for hunting that she established a hunting society.

"I hunted with my husband. I was a good huntress, I hunted rabbits. I used to hunt for wild boar, hunting for partridge, it was splendid. Ah! I keep an indelible memory of it."

Did you have a gun?
"Well, of course. And I didn't miss the target."

It wasn't too heavy a gun?
"No, it was an eighteen. It's for women. It's okay, but heavy all the same. My husband had a twenty; he had the twenty and I had the eighteen. Oh! I was very strong. I had a lot of strength; I was strong in my wrist . . . tremendous."

Did you get on well with Mr. Calment?
"Oh! He was so sweet! Oh! How nice he was! He was sweet! Like his father. His father was sweet. My husband was a marvelous man. When one has an angel one keeps him, and the rest don't see you."

He loved you very much?
"Ah! Very much, very much."

You have had a full life.
"Oh! Yes, a great life. And then, I had character, a lot of character and that helped me a lot. My husband loved my boyish character. It pleased him, that."

Would you have liked to have had a job?
"Well, yes, I would have liked to.

Why would you have liked to?
"To be useful."

Do you remember your daughter's first Communion?
"Ah, even more! Seeing that I remember the baptism. I remember the first Communion even more! It was in a boarding school, a church school. Madame Benet's school, who was . . . . I don't recall any more. At the moment I have a little amnesia, at times. After the ceremony each communicant went back into her family for a big meal. Now, it's the usual."

Do you remember how Yvonne was dressed?
"Of course, for the first Communion! The classic white muslin dress. It was almost an authoritarian shape, almost a uniform. The straight dress in white muslin with lots of frills."

Did she wear a headdress?
"Yes. A wreath of flowers. Oh! Dear, you're asking me a bit too much. When I got married, I had a wreath, a wreath of white lilac. That's when I got married."

How were you dressed that day?
"Well, I had a pink dress at the time, a pretty dress. A fashionable dress of course."

Did you wear hats?

"Oh, yes! One wore hats then! I wore them for a long time. Later, one did away with them."

Your daughter . . .

"Oh, yes! How intelligent. Yes, we had the same taste."

Did she like hunting?

"At the time one didn't think about it. I didn't think about it myself. She liked music, that's all. I played piano duets with her. The usual."

Do you remember her illness?

"We took her to . . . Oh! I don't recall any more."

And was Yvonne ill before having Frederic, or after?

"After. That broke out after, later."

Did she die at home or in the hospital?

"At home. When she came back from the hospital, it was Advent and she came to die at home. Yes. You're reminding me of sad times. No, it's too painful."

I won't talk about it any more.

"No. It's too painful."

You took care of Frederic?

"Naturally! Who takes better care than the grandmother?"

You loved him very much?

"That's a pointless question. He had a particularly good nature, a pleasant nature."

There are people having children without being married. Do you think that's better?

"Oh! No! It's the children who suffer. Ah! Yes! Children suffer because of it. Children are the priority."

Suddenly during the interview, Madame Calment turned the tables and asked Doctor Lebre, who was quizzing her, "Will you be there, doctor, when they put me in the coffin?"

For someone as famous as you, I couldn't do otherwise.

"Then I'm going to ask you a favor."

With pleasure.

"When they put me in the coffin, put the photo of my grandson at my right, and the one of my daughter at my left, and they will be buried with me. Oh, that will only be an imaginary burial, they are both in the ground already, but that way they will be beside me."

There's no indication that Doctor Lebre responded to her during the interview; however, he did carry out her wishes precisely by placing Yvonne's photograph into the coffin on her left side and Frederic's photograph on her right side.

Do you like pastries?
"Not much, no, not much. My husband liked them. I never got excited about pastries. I would eat them, but they didn't excite me."

What other treats do you like?
"Anything sweet. I love sweetness. I have a sweet at every meal. I have a good appetite and a good digestion."

The following session demonstrates Madame Calment's wit, independence, quick-thinking, and her tenacity when Doctor Lebre presses her, perhaps a tad too far.

We have come back to ask you some questions.
"I hear you."

Can you hear me well enough at the moment?
"Um."

Can you hear me well?
"I think I said I can hear you well now!"

Do you know the telephone number here?
"No. I never use it! I'm not used to it."

I will give it to you.
"I don't need it."

I'll give it to you; listen carefully. It's 90 49 29 29. Can you repeat it to me?
"What? I've no idea. Unfortunately, I'm hard of hearing, totally."

Listen. The number is 4, 9, 2, 9, 2, 9.
"You've got it! That's correct."

So, repeat it to me.
"You don't need it. What do you want me to do with this number? What do you want me to do with it? I don't need it. I can't give it to anyone."

You are going to repeat the first figures . . .
"I won't keep it; no, I won't keep it."

So what number is it?
"I can't hear; I hear badly."

You hear when you want to.
"No, I don't remember. No, don't count on it. I repeat: What do you want me to do with it? What do you want me to do with it? I always do what I want. Very determined and scheming, a tiny bit, I scheme."

You still scheme now?

"Bah, when the occasion arises! I've never been shy, no; I'm never shy, arrogant rather. I was never pushed around. I refused. I would react with the quarter hour of salvation, as I used to call it."

Were you religious at the time?

"I still am. I would always go to Mass and on Fridays, I went to vespers, too. I would go the first Friday of the month and there was a ceremony, wasn't there?"

Yes, and do you believe in God now?

"Yes, I believe; all that I ask Him, He grants me. How do you expect me not to believe?"

Do you often think about it?

"What do you want? I need Him. I need Him all the time: I ask Him for this, I ask Him for that."

And you talk to Him?

"Ah! As one talks to God. I don't see Him but when one talks in church, He hears everyone. I ask Him to forgive me. I question Him. When I have something to do I say to Him, 'My God, Lord, I need you more than ever to help me do certain things.' I ask him this service."

You talk with him?

"Yes, well, I, I, I…like a believer. When I had

my operation. When I am in trouble, I ask Him to help me."

What do you want Him to help you with at the moment?

"To live, to live without worry, to live reasonably, to live my life, the little I have to live."

And the thought of God supports you?

"Yes, when there is something, I say to Him, 'My God, help me, my God.' I annoy Him. He gives me satisfaction."

Do you want to die?

"No! Who wants to die? You? But if death comes, it won't bother me."

When someone from the media remarked, *Maybe I'll see you next year*, she shot back, as if she had rehearsed a Johnny Carson punch line, "Why not? You don't seem to be in such bad health."

Following are some of Madame Calment's unsolicited comments recorded by Doctor Lebre during the several years of interviews after she became a celebrity. They shed light on the humor, wit, charm, and positive outlook that must have assisted her through her many years.

"The good Lord must have forgotten me."

"I had fun. I'm having fun."

"I've always had the stomach of an ostrich. When I was younger, I could eat stones."

"I have legs of iron, but to tell you the truth, they're starting to rust and buckle a bit."

"There's no such thing as a terrible ordeal, you just have to find a solution each time."

"I was never very pretty, nor ugly for that matter, and I've improved with age."

"Always kept a smile. I attribute my long life to that. I believe I will die laughing. That's part of my program."

"I see badly, I hear badly, and I feel bad, but everything's fine."

"I'm God's little angel."

"Every age has its happiness and its troubles."

"I lost my husband, my daughter, my grandson, I don't see anymore, I hardly hear, but I don't suffer: therefore, I don't complain."

"I've taken care of my skin with olive oil all my life and just a little puff of powder to finish it off. I never wear mascara; I laugh until I cry too often."

"I've never had more than one wrinkle—and I'm sitting on it."

"I've profited, I profited from advantages that other women don't have."

CHAPTER THIRTEEN

" **J**eanne Calment totally upset certain calculations nearing her 120th birthday; she faced the probability of dying with a value of 100 percent, thus a certainty, which is impossible. First, we have to push back the theoretical value to a minimum of 125 years.

Whatever it is, the case of Madame Calment currently represents the farthest end of human longevity in terms of figures. Each additional day that she lived after 120 years, she was a statistical challenge for scientists. And there she disturbed everyone. Several international conferences have already been devoted to her. The fact that her age has been confirmed and validated obliges all the specialists in this field to take it (and her) seriously. All the curves, all the equations, all the calculations must constantly be reviewed to agree with her!" (Excerpt from the book, *Jeanne Calment From Van Gogh's Time to Ours*)

On her 120th birthday, there was a great celebration at her retirement home, Maison du Lac.

The media began arriving days before and started jostling for favorable television camera positions and perhaps a lucky chance to interview Madame Calment. Crowds milled around outside to honor her and to hopefully steal a quick glance. Why all the fuss over her 120th birthday? The celebration was greater than the year before and would make her 121st birthday pale in comparison.

Doctor Victor Lebre seemed to dwell on her 120th birthday to the exclusion of all others. One could easily conclude that he envisioned her 120th birthday as a unique passage. It was. He made a pact or bet with Madame Calment several years earlier that he would see her 120th birthday. Shortly after her 118th birthday, Doctor Lebre reminded her of their bet. She responded, "Ah! That I doubt." Shortly after her 119th birthday, she told Doctor Lebre, "I promised that I'd live to 120 years. I'll do my best." Perhaps Doctor Lebre sufficiently summed up this remarkable feat when he wrote, "Each additional day that she lived after 120 years, she was a statistical challenge for scientists. And there she disturbed everyone."

Remarkably, there is no evidence to suggest that anyone in the media, friends, physicians, scientists, or anyone who was directly involved with Madame Calment ever connected the magic age of 120 with God's rule. Or, if so, they kept it to themselves. Surely someone among this throng must have known about the 120-year rule. Maybe there were some who were aware of God's 120-year rule but ignored it because of their skeptical view of parts of the Bible as being unrealistic or just a myth. If so, once you step onto that slippery slope and start discarding sections of the Bible to meet your own standards and beliefs, it becomes difficult to discern a stopping point. A correlation could be made with our constitution, wherein portions that seem unrealistic or old fashioned to our elected leaders are ignored. It remains a mystery to me as to why this issue wasn't brought to light, evaluated, and debated at great length.

Many super centenarians are waiting in the wings. Only time will answer this critical question: Maxima 120?

SECRETS TO LONGEVITY

- ೋ Affinity with God
- ೋ Daily exercise
- ೋ Proper nutrition
- ೋ Proper weight
- ೋ Drink adequate amounts of water
- ೋ Adequate sleep
- ೋ Sunny disposition
- ೋ Close family ties
- ೋ Laughter
- ೋ Varied interests such as sports, reading, music
- ೋ Cultivate friends
- ೋ High self-esteem
- ೋ Superb work ethics
- ೋ Annual physical

Most of the suggestions listed above are, of course, not secrets at all. People in general are aware of at least most of them but unfortunately ignore a portion of them or simply succumb due to other pressures. Fortunately, a large investment of money is not required to implement such a program. What you need is determination, concern, and a positive attitude to make this happen. It probably won't be easy. Prepare for great resistance, especially if you have teenagers. But keep in mind, regardless of what they say and their seemingly ungrateful attitude, young people desire and need your adult guidance.

- Attend a church of your choice with your family on a weekly basis. Make sure your actions and words throughout the week meet the high standards demanded by God.

- Daily exercise doesn't require a lot of your valuable time or require a large investment in equipment. If you have a sedentary job, you can exercise at your desk without interfering with your work. While sitting in your chair, lift your legs up so that they extend straight out, then slowly lower them to the floor and repeat. Practice this exercise until you can easily do 50 without stopping. Walk vigorously and avoid elevators. Squeeze balls can strengthen your arms and hands and relieve tension. At home, all you need is a place such as a bedroom or office for situps, pushups, squats, and dumbbell exercises. Your physical condition determines your starting point. This might be a good time for your annual physical and consultation with your doctor about your exercise and weight control plan. If you're out-of-shape, start slowly and work toward a goal, a realistic number established by you and perhaps your physician. A set of inexpensive dumbbells appropriate for you sex, size, and age can be used to tone the upper body and burn a few calories. At least once a week, and preferably twice a week, exercise very vigorously— exercise that makes you perspire. Most people need about thirty minutes to achieve a "runners-high" condition. Jogging or pushing a lawn mower will do the trick. If you jog, you should purchase a good pair of medium priced shoes but other clothes designed specifically for jogging is expensive and unnecessary. The squats mentioned earlier may be accomplished by extending both arms outward from your side, then squat until the backs of your legs touch the calves of your legs. Rise up to a standing position and repeat. Set a goal of a few each day, and gradually increase to at least 50 squats per workout. If your child's school doesn't have a physical education program that lasts for at least one hour each day, push for one.

- Proper nutrition begins by ignoring the purchase of expensive junk food at the grocery store, regardless of the pressure from toddlers or teenagers. If junk food is not in the home, that solves the problem at home. Instead, buy less expensive fruit and place it in a bowl that is accessible to all. Most likely it will be ignored at first, but eventually a taste will be developed for most fruits. Granted, with both parents working it's tempting in the evening to order out for calorie- and fat-laden pizza or similar foods. Set a goal and stick to it that a sit-down evening meal will be served that is well balanced and nutritious, with an abundance of fresh vegetables. If possible, involve the entire family in meal preparation. Children can assist by doing less complicated duties, such as setting the table or preparing the salad. If meal preparation every day is absolutely not practical for your family, check out the many locations that have recognized this problem and sell well balanced meals that you can purchase and take home to eat. Although this is not the primary goal, you will probably notice a decrease in money spent on food.

At most schools, students are able to purchase junk food from machines on school property, and many school cafeterias are laden with unhealthy and fattening junk food. Pressure from the PTA and other interested organizations should be brought against education administrators to cease and desist the fattening of our children. Obesity can result in cardiovascular diseases and dreaded diabetes, even in youngsters. If you need a refresher course in what proper nutrition consists of, check out a book at your local library on this subject or visit the USDA's Nutrition Education web site.

- If an adequate exercise program and proper nutrition is maintained, weight should eventually stabilize. Exercise alone usually won't do the trick. You would have to jog a considerable distance to burn off the calories in one doughnut. If you need to lose weight, eat small portions. Chew the food thoroughly. Eat slowly and carry on a conversation. You will be amazed at how great nutritious food can taste when eaten in this manner. And forget those crash diets, amazing pills, and expensive diet food programs with which we are constantly bombarded from every corner of the media. They seldom work.

- Drink plenty of water, but don't force yourself to drink. If you exercise properly, your body will thirst for water. Soft drinks or other fluids will never be an adequate substitute for water. They won't quench your thirst like water. Bottled water might be the in thing, but it's expensive and unnecessary. Public drinking water is regulated by the EPA, whereas bottled water is regulated by the FDA. Generally, over the years, the FDA has adopted the EPA's standards for tap water as standards for bottled water. Standards for contaminants in tap water and bottled water are very similar but not the same. Not all bottled water contains fluoride, which promotes strong teeth and prevents or reduces tooth decay. If you use only bottled water that doesn't contain fluoride, you should advise your dentist.

The nine secrets mentioned above are self-explanatory and comments are unnecessary.

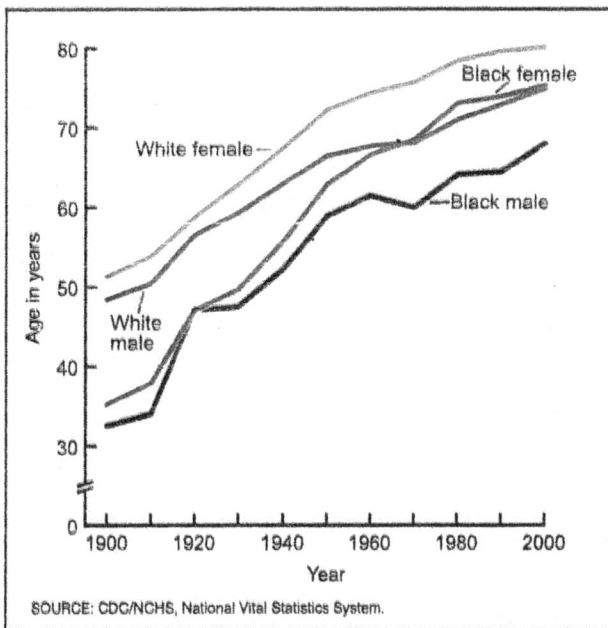

Figure 1. Life expectancy at birth by race and sex:
Death-registration states, 1900–1902 to 1919–1921, and
United States, 1929–1931 to 1999–2001

Courtesy United States decennial life tables, United States life
tables. National vital statistics reports, Hyattsville, MD;
National Center for Health Statistics, 2008.

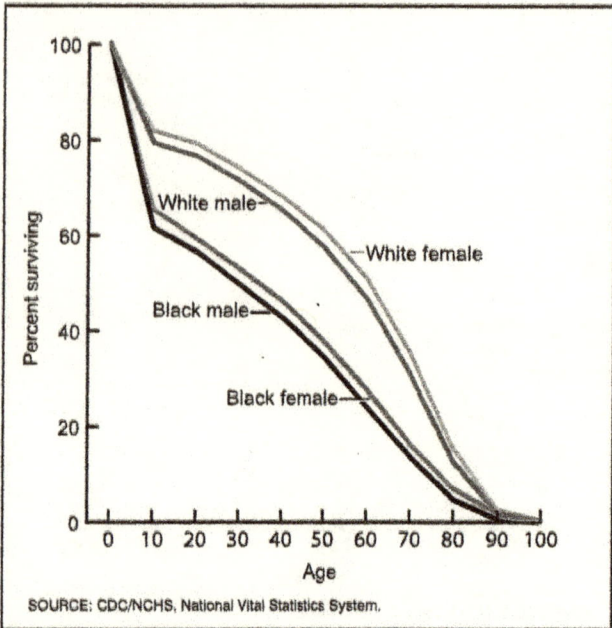

Figure 2. Percentage surviving by age, race, and sex: Death-registration states, 1900–1902

Courtesy United States decennial life tables, United States life tables. National vital statistics reports, Hyattsville, MD; National Center for Health Statistics, 2008.

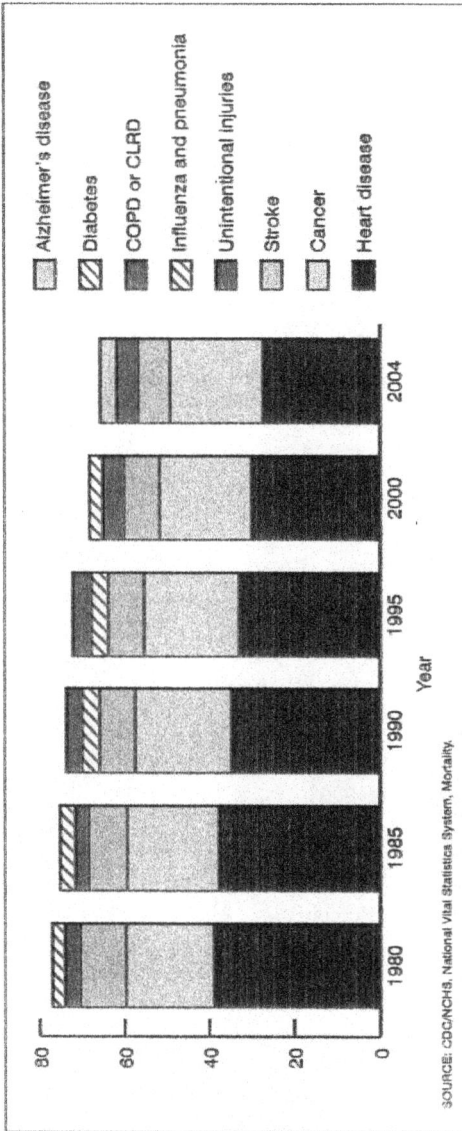

Figure 3. Percentage of total deaths for the top five causes of death among females: 1980–2004

SOURCE: CDC/NCHS, National Vital Statistics System, Mortality.

Courtesy United States decennial life tables, United States life tables. National vital statistics reports, Hyattsville, MD; National Center for Health Statistics, 2008.

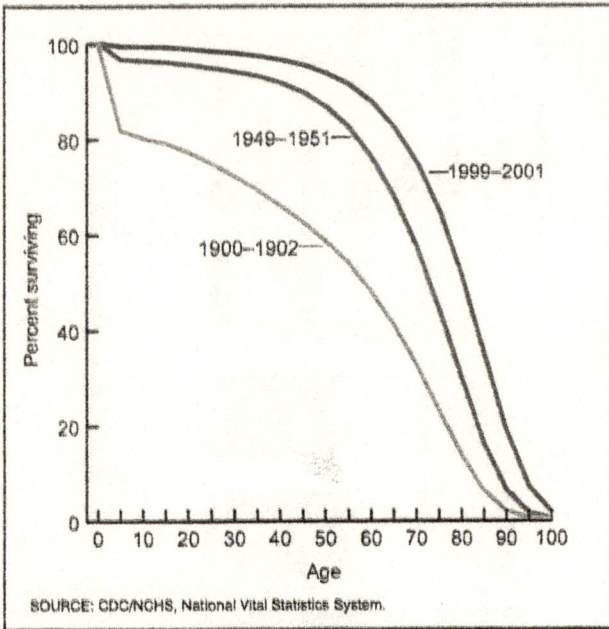

Figure 4. Percentage surviving by age: Death-registration states, 1900–1902, and United States, 1949–1951 and 1999–2001

Courtesy United States decennial life tables, United States life tables. National vital statistics reports, Hyattsville, MD; National Center for Health Statistics, 2008.

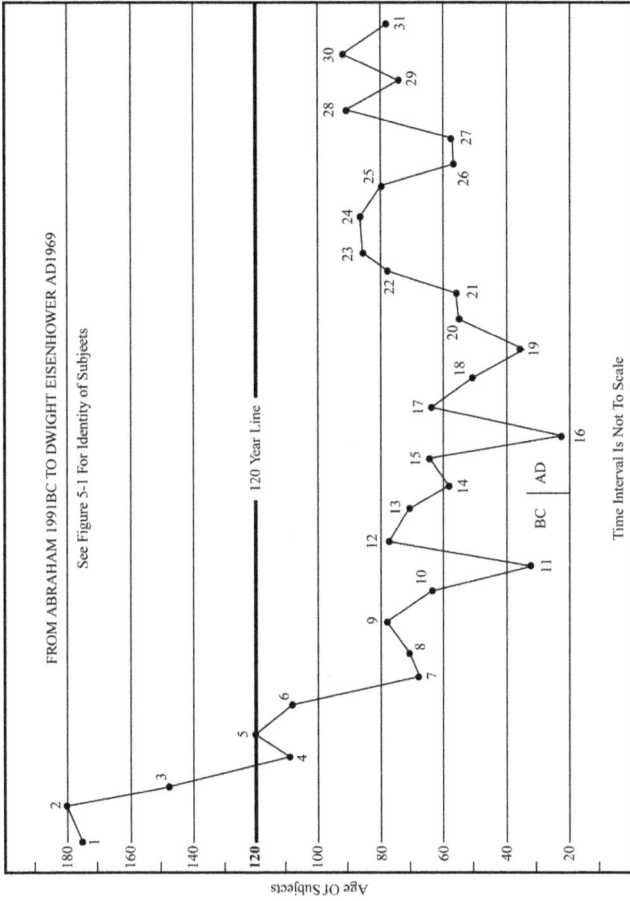

FROM ABRAHAM 1991BC TO DWIGHT EISENHOWER AD1969

See Figure 5-1 For Identity of Subjects

120 Year Line

Age Of Subjects

BC | AD

Time Interval Is Not To Scale

Figure 5

83

BIRTHS AND DEATHS BC

NAME	BORN	DIED	AGE
1. Abraham	2166	1991	175
2. Isaac	2066	1886	180
3. Jacob	2006	1859	147
4. Joseph	1915	1805	110
5. Moses	1526	1406	120
6. Joshua	1280	1390	110
7. David	1037	970	67
8. Socrates	469	399	70
9. Plato	427	348	78
10. Aristotle	384	322	62
11. Alexander the Great	356	323	32
12. Archimedes	287	212	75
13. Herod the Great	73	4	69

Jesus Born **BIRTHS AND DEATHS AD**

NAME	BORN	DIED	AGE
14. Herod Antipas	20BC	AD39	59
15. Constantine the Great	272	337	65
16. Flavius Claudius Constantinus	317	340	23
17. Saint Bede	673	735	62
18. Alfred the Great	849	899	50
19. Saint Francis Assisi	1191	1226	35
20. Geoffrey Chancer	1345	1400	55
21. Christopher Columbus	1451	1506	55
22. Galileo	1564	1642	78
23. Isaac Newton	1642	1727	85
24. Benjamin Franklin	1706	1790	84
25. Charles Barbage	1792	1871	79
26. Ludwig van Beethoven	1770	1827	57
27. George Washington	1742	1799	57
28. Florence Nightingale	1820	1910	90
29. Louis Pasteur	1822	1895	73
30. Winston Churchill	1874	1965	91
31. Dwight Eisenhower	1890	1969	79

Figure 5-1

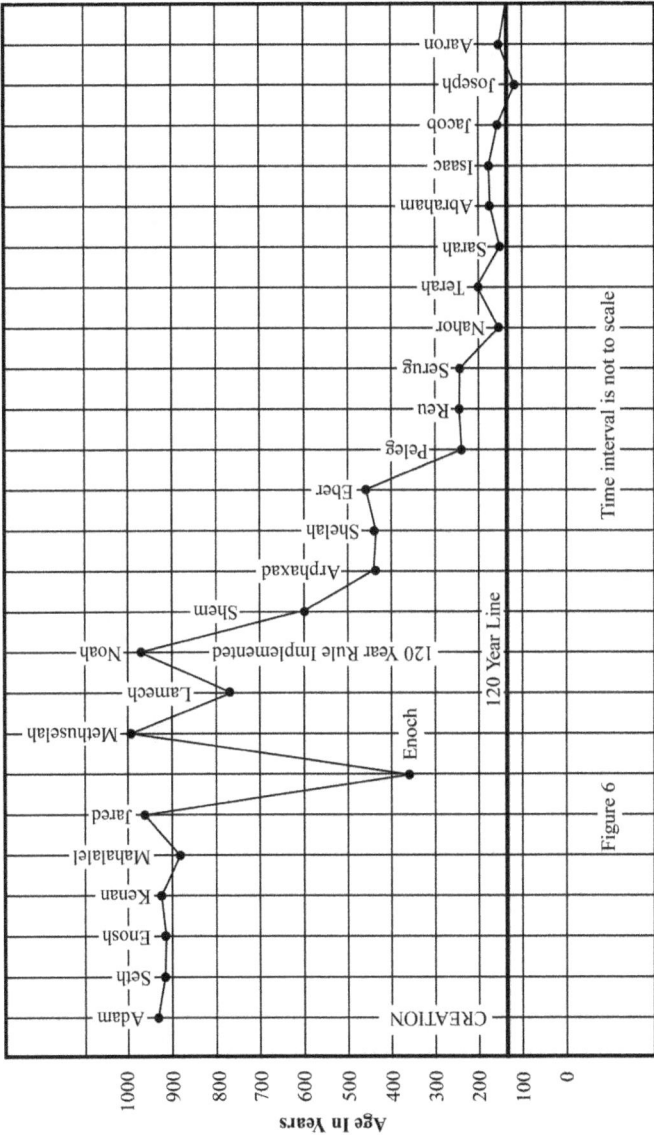

Figure 6

Time interval is not to scale

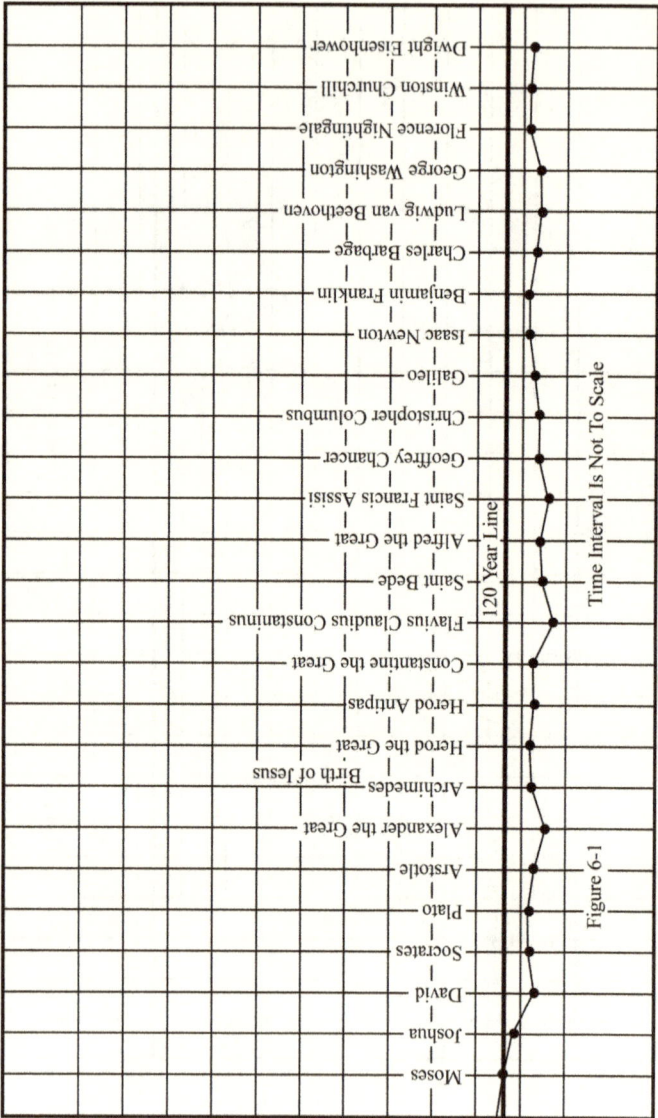

Dwight Eisenhower

Winston Churchill

Florence Nightingale

George Washington

Ludwig van Beethoven

Charles Babbage

Benjamin Franklin

Isaac Newton

Galileo

Christopher Columbus

Geoffrey Chaucer

Saint Francis Assisi

Alfred the Great

Saint Bede

Flavius Claudius Constaninus

Constantine the Great

Herod Antipas

Herod the Great

Birth of Jesus

Archimedes

Alexander the Great

Aristotle

Plato

Socrates

David

Joshua

Moses

120 Year Line

Time Interval Is Not To Scale

Figure 6-1

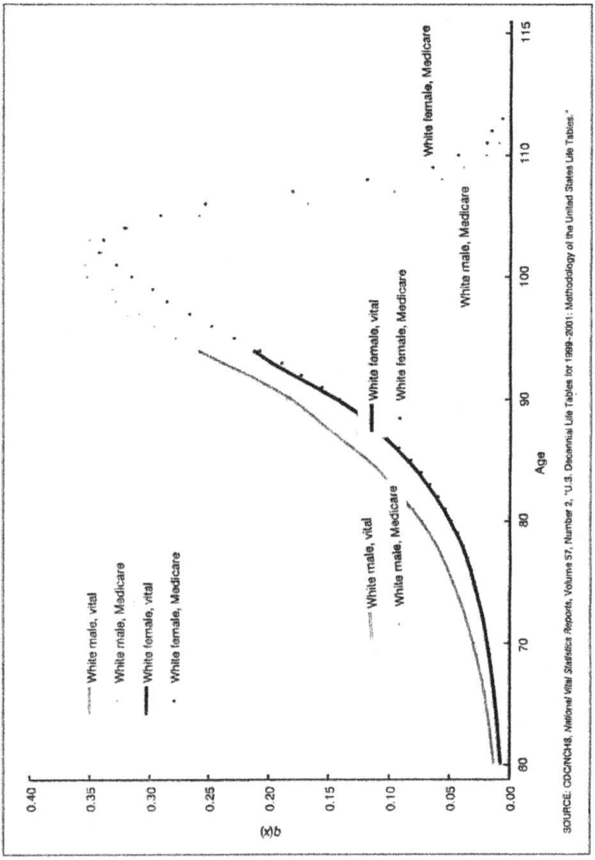

Figure 7: Comparison of probabilities of dying ($q(x)$) from vital statistics data (1999–2001) and Medicare data (1999–2001) in the white population

SOURCE: CDC/NCHS, National Vital Statistics Reports, Volume 57, Number 2, "U.S. Decennial Life Tables for 1999–2001: Methodology of the United States Life Tables."

Courtesy United States decennial life tables, United States life tables. National vital statistics reports, Hyattsville, MD; National Center for Health Statistics, 2008.

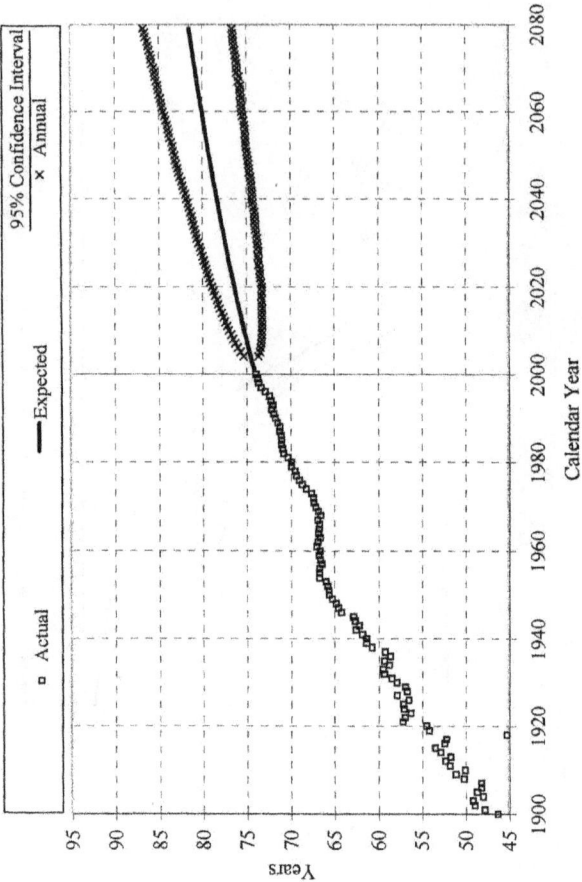

Figure 8. —Male Period Life Expectancies at Birth, Calendar Years 1900–2078

Courtesy United States decennial life tables, United States life tables. National vital statistics reports, Hyattsville, MD; National Center for Health Statistics, 2008.

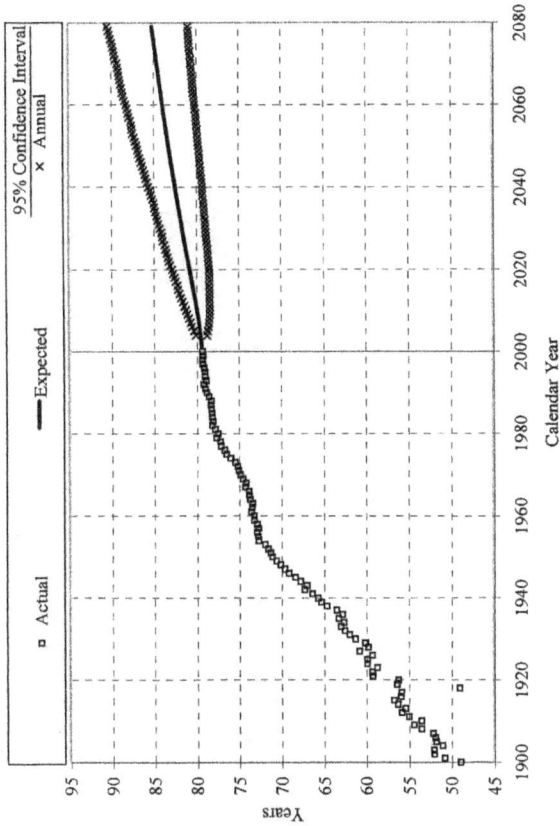

Figure 9. — Female Period Life Expectancies at Birth, Calendar Years 1900-2078

Courtesy United States decennial life tables, United States life tables. National vital statistics reports, Hyattsville, MD; National Center for Health Statistics, 2008.

Charles D. Richardson

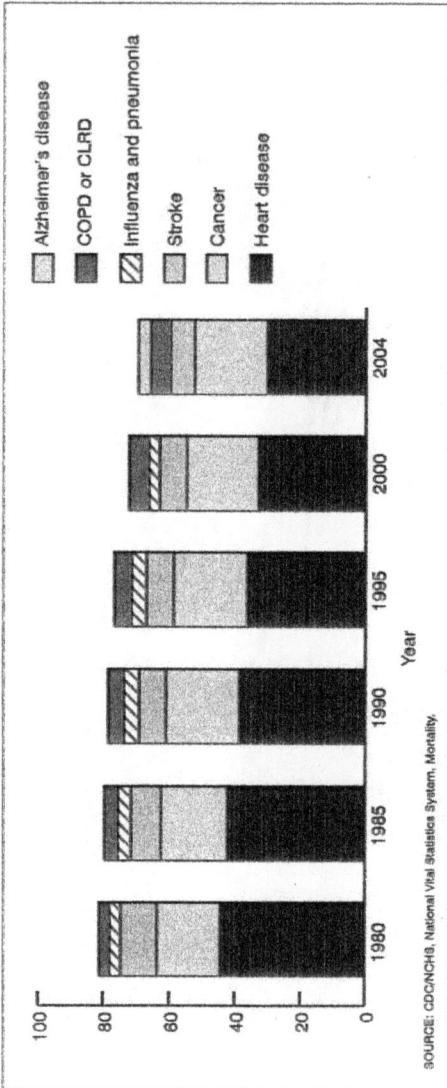

Figure 10. Percentage of total deaths for the top five causes of death among all races, 65 years of age and over: 1980–2004

SOURCE: CDC/NCHS, National Vital Statistics System, Mortality.

Courtesy United States decennial life tables, United States life tables. National vital statistics reports, Hyattsville, MD; National Center for Health Statistics, 2008.

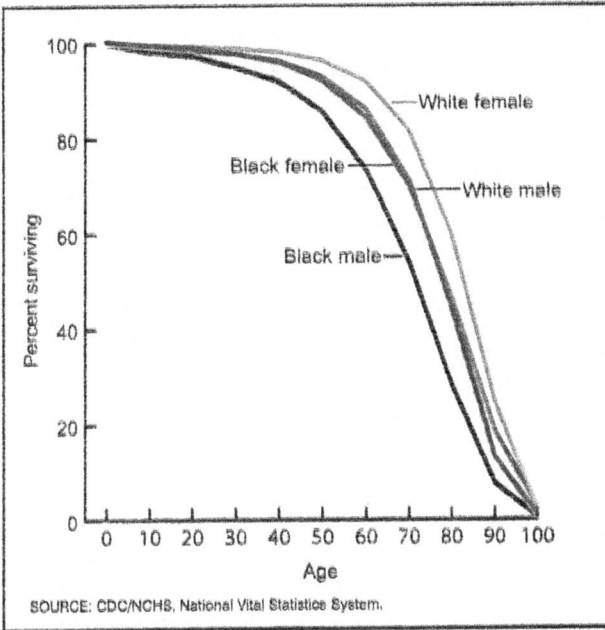

Figure 11. Percentage surviving by age, race, and sex: United States, 1999–2001

Courtesy United States decennial life tables, United States life tables. National vital statistics reports, Hyattsville, MD; National Center for Health Statistics, 2008.

www.ingramcontent.com/pod-product-compliance
Lightning Source LLC
Chambersburg PA
CBHW051841040426
42447CB00006B/640